Praise for *Having It All ... and Making It Work:*

"This is not just another intimidating book on balancing your life—it is an approachable, realistic look at the age-old question: which comes first: family or career? Its solutions are practical, hopeful, and principled."

—Dr. Stephen R. Covey,
author, *The 7 Habits of Highly Effective People*

"I like this concept of balance because it takes into account the reality of conflicting priorities. When your work and family are both very important to you, as they are to me and most of my professional friends, how do you cope? I've opted for a work situation that allows me to be very involved with my wife in the challenging role of parenting."

—Steve Young,
ESPN Broadcaster and two-time NFL MVP

"Work/life balance is one of the most daunting personal challenges that individual managers face today. Mills, Mattu, and Hornby have done an exceptional job in putting together a very readable and practical guide to overcoming that challenge—and turning the frustration of imbalance into the joy of balance."

—Oren Harari, Ph.D.,
author of *The Leadership Secrets of Colin Powell*

"One hour with this book can make a lifetime of difference. The authors offer a practical framework with useful insights on managing the conflicting priorities of work and family."

—Joel Shulman,
Associate Professor, and Robert Weissman
Term Chair of Entrepreneurship, Babson College

"I am impressed with this book and plan to use it in my courses on Organizational Leadership. It will be an important addition to our curriculum. My students will be well served by such wisdom."

—MICHAEL QUIGLEY,
Professor of Organizational Leadership, Brevard College

"This is wise counsel for anyone who wants a fully engaged life. It is possibility thinking turned into life-enhancing action planning. If heeded, it could change your life. If heeded by many it could change workplace norms. Read it and pass it on."

—LOIS A. VITT, PH.D.,
Founding Director, Institute for Socio-Financial
Studies and mother of six grown children

"*Having It All... and Making It Work* is both simple and profound. It provides practical tips, tools, and guidelines to help professionals have a better life and achieve what is really important."

—MARSHALL GOLDSMITH,
described in *Fast Company* as America's preeminent executive coach,
in *Forbes* as one of five most respected executive coaches,
and in *The Wall Street Journal* as one of the top ten executive educators

Having It All...
and Making
It Work

Having It All... and Making It Work

Six Steps
for Putting Both Your Career
and Your Family First

D. Quinn Mills
Harvard Business School

Sasha K. Mattu
Harvard Business School

Kirstin R. Hornby
Harvard Business School

An Imprint of PEARSON EDUCATION
Upper Saddle River, NJ • New York • London • San Francisco • Toronto • Sydney
Tokyo • Singapore • Hong Kong • Cape Town • Madrid
Paris • Milan • Munich • Amsterdam

www.ft-ph.com

Library of Congress Catalogine-in-Publication Data

Mills, Daniel Quinn.
    Having it all...and making it work: six steps for putting both your career and your
family first./D. Quinn Mills, Sasha K. Mattu, Kirstin R. Hornby
      p. cm.
    ISBN 0-13-144022-5
    1. Work and family. I. Mattu, Sasha K. II. Hornby, Kirstin R.
    III. Title. IV. Series

HD4904.25M55 2004
650.1—dc22   2003062417

Editorial/production supervision: *Kerry Reardon*
Cover design director: *Jerry Votta*
Cover design: *Mary Jo DeFranco*
Art director: *Gail Cocker-Bogusz*
Manufacturing manager: *Alexis Heydt-Long*
Manufacturing buyer: *Maura Zaldivar*
Executive editor: *Jim Boyd*
Editorial assistant: *Richard Winkler*
Marketing director: *John Pierce*
Marketing manager: *Laura Bulcher*
Full-service production manager: *Anne R. Garcia*

 © 2004 Pearson Education, Inc.
Publishing as Prentice Hall
Upper Saddle River, NJ 07458

Prentice Hall offers excellent discounts on this book when ordered in quantity for bulk
purchases or special sales. For more information, please contact: U.S. Corporate and
Government Sales, 1-800-382-3419, corpsales@pearsontechgroup.com. For sales outside
of the U.S., please contact: International Sales, 1-317-581-3793,
international@pearsontechgroup.com

Printed in the United States of America

First printing

ISBN 0-13-144022-5

Pearson Education LTD.
Pearson Education Australia Pty., Limited
Pearson Education Singapore, Pte. Ltd.
Pearson Education North Asia Ltd.
Pearson Education Canada, Ltd.
Pearson Educación de Mexico, S.A. de C.V.
Pearson Education–Japan
Pearson Education Malaysia, Pte. Ltd.

To Shirley Elizabeth Mills
who asked that this book be written.

Contents

Contents

Introduction: *Why Read this Book*

You wouldn't be reading this book if you weren't looking for an answer to the riddle of how to best manage the demands of your work and your personal life.

Many books address the challenge of having both a career and family; however, most of them focus on describing work-life balance in terms of social, gender, historical, and economic factors—rarely getting around to what to do about the problem.

This book focuses on a specific solution to the challenge of balancing career and family.

Having It All...and Making It Work

Our objective is to help empower you to create your own work–family balance by offering a very user-friendly action plan. We believe that defining a problem is not the same as solving it. Thus, we have chosen to speculate on the problem only as much as necessary to understand better what we can do about it.

We briefly define the work-family balance challenge in this *Introduction*; then our book is geared toward six proactive steps we can take individually. This focus facilitates a simple action plan for achieving work–family balance.

Our goal is very simple: To help people find balance in their lives between career and family. To do this, we provide a focused six-step process:

- ■ **Step 1.** Commit to wanting both a career and family: *Rethinking your priorities.*

- ■ **Step 2.** Pursue a process that creates balance: *Balancing what is most important to you.*

- ■ **Step 3.** Make choices and accept the consequences: *Giving up what you don't want badly enough.*

- ■ **Step 4.** Choose a career that supports balance: *Making your balance real.*

- ■ **Step 5.** Involve your loved ones in creating balance: *Refining your balance.*

■ **Step 6.** Review your balance to retain or regain it: *Balance is a destination.*

Why this goal? Because we have discovered that many working professionals and emerging leaders struggle to achieve balance. We also see evidence that chronic imbalance causes serious problems at work and at home.

Sadly, some people live in denial, at least until they experience a major wakeup call. They believe that problems in their personal lives with marriage and family relationships won't affect their work or that problems at work won't affect their family lives, but invariably an imbalance in one domain affects the other.

Each chapter in this book consists of a series of personal stories and essential tips necessary to carry out each crucial step.

Who Are We?

We feel that the most effective way to address the challenge of work and family balance is to include the perspectives of many people—those who are at the cusp of embarking on a career track and starting a family, those who are juggling the demands of both worlds, and also those who are at the end of their career phase and whose children have left home.

In preparing the content and ideas of this book, we worked with hundreds of professional people who are trying to achieve balance in their own lives. We interacted with them personally and discovered how they are grappling with balance in their own lives, and we learned much of value from their successes and their failures.

The diversity of those we worked with in preparing this book is reflected in us, the authors, and we want to share with you our motivation and interest in writing this book.

Quinn Mills

I have been a professor at the Harvard Business School for many years. Many of my friends are now far along in their careers and have deep regrets about how little of themselves they shared with their spouses and with their children as they were growing up. They wish they had attained a better balance in their lives.

Many of my students have told me that they are afraid that the same thing will happen to them—that years from now they'll finish their careers with deep regret about all they missed of family life. But other students have an entirely different concern—that in a few years they'll feel compelled to abandon promising careers in order to have a family. They fear the sort of imbalance that means giving up a career to have a family.

People struggle so much with these issues that they frequently retreat into illusions about them, promising themselves that if they do this or that, they'll somehow find the balance that is otherwise so difficult to attain.

I spoke at length to the people who were said to be most successful at achieving balance and with others who had failed and were consumed with bitterness and regret.

From conversations, reading, observation, and life experience, I created a unique approach to achieving balance. I wrote this book to share this approach with you, hoping that you might find balance in your own lives. I hope that you will take away from this book the conviction that balance is possible and that you can change your life to make balance a reality for you and your loved ones.

I have had the personal blessing of wonderful children and have struggled with balance between career and family for many years. Several of the techniques in this book I discovered in my personal life and found them effective; some I learned from others. Finding proper balance is one of the most important things in each of our lives today.

Sasha Mattu

When I was younger, I never thought of having a family as a choice—it was just something that was part of my picture of success. I didn't feel that I was asking for too much. It simply seemed that this was the way it was supposed to be if I just worked hard enough.

Having played professional tennis, then graduating from Harvard, I realized that to maintain this kind of career intensity, I needed to make different choices to include a family in my life. I did not know that a rewarding career and loving family would compete for the same limited resources—my time and energy.

The fanatic 100% dedication that it takes for me to be successful professionally is now the same definition that I have for my family—100% dedication of myself. How can I do both? Certainly, 100% to career + 100% to family = burnout or blowout.

I have asked professionals around me who have both a career and family, and I have been overwhelmed by the spectrum of solutions I have seen. I was disappointed to find that many were still in the process of figuring it out for themselves—what does this mean for me with 20 years less experience? I then sought answers in books and found that most just defined the problem and didn't tell me how I can create this balance for myself.

Introduction: Why Read this Book

I hope that this book is a tool for other young people who are about to set out on a career, who are ambitious, hopeful, but who need guidance in thinking about the long road ahead. There are pitfalls that can sometimes be avoided if one is aware of them early on. This book is about life and its pitfalls, and more importantly, what to do about them. The pages that follow address the major pitfalls in our lives and the dangers of burnout and blowout.

Kirstin Hornby

I'm at an age when I must make decisions about how to structure my career and family. As I think about these issues, I have observed people around me, such as my parents and my colleagues—those who spend too much time at work and not enough with their families, and those who have given up their careers to have a family.

I have also noticed people around me who are struggling to juggle both career and family. I have heard dozens of stories about women who've had to drop off a career track to have a family and who couldn't get back on, and about those who realized they wanted to have a family, but it was too late. I've heard stories about dual-income families struggling to find time for everything and stories about divorced parents who can barely keep life together. I've begun to wonder whether there is any way to balance family and career so that one doesn't have to be sacrificed for the other.

I chose to research and write this book to help both others and myself by discovering whether balance is really possible. I learned that we cannot necessarily have everything in exactly the way we might have imagined, but that by looking at balance in a new way, it is possible to have both a happy family and a successful career.

A Chinese proverb tells us that a journey of a thousand miles begins with a single step. For us, the first step is a commitment to wanting both a career and a family. We invite you to join us in the journey.

Acknowledgments

We are deeply grateful to Jim Boyd and Ken Shelton, our editors, for their insightful contributions to this book. We are also grateful to the Harvard Business School Division of Research for its support in the research that is the basis for this book.

Quinn Mills
Kirstin Hornby
Sasha Mattu

Commit to Wanting Both a Career and Family:
Rethinking Your Priorities

You may feel at times that you must choose between having a successful career and having a great personal and family life. But we believe, based on our extensive research and personal life experience, that you can have both. You need not trade off your top priorities. Step 1 is an invitation to exercise the faith and courage to commit to wanting both a career and family.

Having It All...and Making It Work

The tragedy of September 11, 2001 and the ongoing threat of terrorism highlight the need for each of us to rethink our priorities—to ask ourselves:

- Do we really understand what is most important in our lives?

- Are we giving these priorities all the time and attention they deserve?

As we reevaluate our lives, we look to our home environment for meaning, security, and comfort. Our vulnerability is being exposed, even magnified, and we want now more than ever to have meaningful and significant relationships in our lives.

Simultaneously, our careers continue to be more demanding than ever before, having a huge impact on the family unit. We see more latchkey children than ever before, a greater need for childcare support, and the highest rate of fast-food consumption in history. The ambition for career success has eroded the quality of family life.

The economic boom of the late 1990s was a time when careers took precedence for many people. This was followed by a national tragedy and a national economic recession that displaced many professionals and disrupted business in general. After September 11, many people returned to their families for meaning.

Step 1

Those of us who have careers must ask whether we are short-changing our families by giving more time and attention to our careers. Are we rationalizing our commitment to our careers at the expense of our loved ones? Or are we sacrificing career success, perhaps even plateauing prematurely at an early stage, in order to devote more time to family and other priorities?

How can we attain both career and family success? In these two areas, making tradeoffs is unacceptable.

JONATHAN'S STORY

Can I have it all? I found it remarkable how such a simple question could trigger such diverse and complex emotions in me. As I've continued to ask myself this question over the course of the last several years, I've often thought back to my childhood. If asked the question then, I would have responded with a resounding "Yes!" I had two parents who loved me, I excelled in school and on the athletic field, and I had more friends than I knew what to do with. What else was there? I truly thought I had it all.

However, life has continued to teach me that its very nature is much more complex than the confines of childhood achievement. I've broadened my horizons with global experiences, spent years in the military, and started a family of my own. I've seen that life doesn't always reward hard work, patience, and faith—but it often does. I've seen the untimely death of loved ones, divorce, drug abuse, political and corporate corruption, the violence of political and religious struggles around the world—but I also realize that darkness lies often in the shadows of the good things in life. So, can a person really have it all in a world that is defined by shades of gray, rather than lines of black and white? My answer is now a resounding "Yes, if life is approached the right way!"

Jonathan is no longer a young man. He's lived through important experiences, suffered losses, has a spouse and young children, and is asking himself what he can expect from life. He wants both a successful career and a loving family, and he believes he can have both.

As children, we are boundless in our imagination and wants, and we believe that we don't have any limitations in our ability to do anything and to gain the benefits at all times. Jonathan told us above how his views changed as he grew up.

Step 1

We ask what Jonathan asks. As we examine our own lives, do we believe we can have it all? And we should answer as Jonathan does, that if we approach life in the right way, we can really have it all.

Family and work are the two most important priorities in the lives of many of us, but we seemingly don't know how to reconcile them, and this causes tremendous stress and frustration. Discovering a method of reconciling the two would contribute to our peace of mind.

Which "first things" do we put first? We often receive the advice to "put first things first." We can do this, but the challenge arises when we have two or more first things— two or more things that are important in our lives and none of which we can set aside for the others.

We then have a conflict between two or more top-priority components of our lives. Having a fulfilling career takes up a lot of time in a person's life, and having a family is also a tremendous challenge. We want both, and we don't want to give up one for the other. The inherent tension—if not outright conflict—between career and family is very real and problematic, and it needs to be resolved.

This is an important comparison. How can we choose between these two areas of our lives when each offers us so much?

Having It All...and Making It Work

Professional/Work vs. Personal/Family

Conflict or Balance?

Job/career	Significant other/spouse
Employees/colleagues	Children/friends
Investments of money	Investments of heart
Work projects	Family projects
Work socials	Family socials/recreation
Sense of success	Sense of belonging
Financial security	Emotional security
Possessions/things	Passions/people
Material goods	Emotional wealth
Helping many, a little	Helping a few, a lot
Intellectual satisfaction	Personal satisfaction
Challenge/excitement	Contentment/peace of mind
Market value	Self-worth

Step 1

The key to our peace of mind and quality of life is found in our wisdom in answering the question, *How do we balance our families and our careers?* Or if we have one and not the other—or neither—how do we set out on a course of life that will give us both without also giving us the intolerable conflicts between the two?

We usually don't have a problem with balance if we are prepared to put career before family or family before career. It's when we can't "put first things first"—when we can't prioritize family over work or work over family because they both come smack dab on the top of our lists. Balance becomes an issue when family and career are equally crucial to our happiness and sense of success.

The Leadership Challenge

Being successful in our chosen fields—whether in business, health care, education, athletics, or any other profession—requires a devotion and love for a career that makes balancing professional passion and commitment with family passion and commitment particularly challenging. Whether we aspire to success or have been successful for some time, the dilemma of meeting the time demands in an increasingly competitive market makes the dilemma of juggling work and family especially poignant.

Having It All...and Making It Work

Success does complicate life by adding many demands in our career lives: We have employees, customers, and suppliers to consider, in addition to bosses. The demands of all these stakeholders add stress. There are likely to be more meetings, more travel, more negotiations, more conflict, and more need for conflict resolution. There are requirements of public appearances, speaking engagements, and public relations. There are the additional temptations of power, wealth, position, and status if we are successful, and to be successful, we devote more time. Then there's less time for our families and more risk of getting badly out of balance.

Notwithstanding the additional demands of a successful career, we believe this:

> **_Being successful is an asset, not a liability, in trying to have both a family and career._**

This is because for many of us, the great value of a profession is that it gives us the opportunity to exercise some independent _leadership_. This exercise of personal leadership distinguishes having a profession from having a mere job in which we put in our time, hoping to get free as soon as possible to return to more important matters.

Leadership helps us fulfill ourselves. It makes us more interesting people and means that we have more to give our families, if only we can find the proper balance so that our careers don't crowd out our families.

The qualities and skills necessary to engage in a rewarding career are also needed in developing a stable family, and vice versa. In essence, finding a better balance between both worlds—career and family—will ultimately make us better at both.

Our Definition of Balance

We know that it is possible to have both a successful career and meaningful family life, and that for most of us, life is only truly fulfilling when we achieve both. Balance is the way in which we can achieve this—to get a lot of what is most important to us.

Balance requires a process.

We don't get into balance at one time and stay there indefinitely; it takes continual vigilance and effort to maintain our balance. This is because life is always changing, and each change raises new threats to our balance.

For example, suppose you get a promotion at the office, which is great, but with it comes additional demands on your time. How will you balance these demands with the needs of your family? Alternatively, you and your spouse have another child. Suddenly, there is much more demand on your time at home. How will you balance these demands with those of your career?

Balance is the process of adjusting to change in a way that keeps the two most important things in your life—your family and your career—in the right relationship to each other, so that neither gets lost in the lurch. Because of the changes that continually impact our lives, balance can be maintained only by close and continual attention and effort. Thus, balance is a process, not a state of being.

We are not suggesting that balance is a blanket solution. Balance won't give you *everything* that you want in terms of your career and family, but with balance . . .

You can have MUCH of what you really want—
and less of what you don't want—
in your life and work.

Balance decreases the guilt, tension, pain, and regret that are created when the two worlds of career and family conflict with each other. As a result, balance allows us to be more emotionally present when at work and when at home.

Achieving a satisfying balance between your personal life and work will make you better at both.

Balance is a mixture of career and family engagement, which gives a person fulfillment and avoids tension, guilt, and regret.

This is not to say that people who don't want families or don't pursue a career can't be happy. If a person has no interest in a career—or a family—that's fine, so long as he or she is satisfied with that choice.

For example, a stay-at-home mom who does volunteer work could be satisfied, or someone who chooses not to be married and instead devotes himself or herself entirely to a career could also be satisfied.

But we must be careful in making decisions of this nature about our lives. For most people today, satisfaction in life requires both family and career, and people who choose one over the other or one and not the other early in adult life often find themselves regretting bitterly later in life what they've given up.

Unless a person knows herself or himself very well, she or he should be careful about choosing career or family above the other. Most people will probably want to have both and should make balancing the two a key part of their strategy for a happy life.

Balance may not be an even 50/50 split between career and family. Some people may feel balanced with 60% career and 40% family emphasis, whereas others may choose to put more emphasis on family. You can determine this for yourself as you follow the six steps in this book to create your own balance.

Critical Success Factors in Rethinking Your Priorities

The critical success factors in rethinking priorities and achieving balance include:

■ Think hard about what you really value and what you really want: **Liking something isn't good enough—you have to really want it**.

■ Try to imagine how you'll feel a number of years from now if you have given up family for career or if you've given up career for family. Then go the way your heart tells you.

■ Take responsibility for being proactive about attaining and maintaining balance.

■ Make a list of priorities that clarify what is most important in work and home life, and be sure you make time for them.

12

Pursue a Process that Creates Balance: *Balancing What Is Most Important to You*

You don't achieve balance by accident but rather by pursuing a process that includes setting priorities, gaining perspective, and establishing boundaries and internal benchmarks. Bottom line: You need to define career and family success in your own terms and balance what is more important to you.

How might we achieve a satisfying balance between our work and family activities? And how, by balancing the things that are most important to us, might we have more time and energy for each? In this chapter, we address these important questions.

Having It All...and Making It Work

First, we need to face a simple fact of life:

Balance won't happen on its own;
we have to create it.

Although this fact of life might be considered a "blinding flash of the obvious," it is still one that escapes many otherwise bright and capable people, and even many leaders. One reason for this oversight may be the trend toward employers, especially large corporations, taking more initiative in helping employees with the management of their work–life balance. Indeed, many professionals now expect that their employers will dispense "life balance" as a benefit of employment.

Certain leaders have taken this trend a giant step further and enlisted a cadre of assistants to help them manage their personal and family lives. It's as though they feel they can delegate or relegate family matters as they would other duties.

Other professionals simply assume that ideas and methods for balancing work and family priorities would come along as needed and that the people and things in their lives would just naturally take care of themselves. Consider Jason's story:

Step 2

JASON'S STORY

I had always thought I would somehow stumble upon the right balance; I assumed that career, family, and community involvement were all important to me and that I would adjust the allocation of my time among these priorities whenever I needed to. I later realized that if I weren't proactive about finding the right balance for me, more than likely, work would come to dominate my life—especially because I enjoy competing with others to make the biggest impact in my firm.

Jason had made a common mistake. He'd thought that balance would somehow evolve on its own as he juggled his priorities. In fact, this is one of the most crucial mistakes we can make. We think that life will work itself out correctly without careful thought and effort, but it won't. We won't be able to balance our lives correctly unless we work at it consciously.

Jason initially took a haphazard approach to having balance. Whatever was urgent at the moment was allotted the greatest time, and it wasn't long before Jason realized that work came to dominate all of his other commitments, including his family.

Having It All...and Making It Work

We all know that "the squeaky wheel gets the grease." It seems that work had a much louder voice than Jason's family commitments. Family was equally important to Jason, but when it came to allotting time, his work was incredibly forceful in making demands on him.

Our work voice can cry loudly about deadlines and deliverables, whereas our family members and matters often suffer in silence. And because our work "puts bread on the table," we tend to listen to and obey its loud voice.

It can happen to any of us. Our work can be a trump card in that it will take precedence over all other aspects of our lives—including family—if we are not careful.

We must choose to be proactive about having balance in our lives by taking responsibility for creating our own balance or imbalance.

We must be aware that the opposite can also occur: Our family can also play the trump card. Indeed, when there is illness, injury, disruption, teenage rebellion, strained marital relationships, or other trouble at home, these personal matters can easily push any and all work—even the most pressing matters—aside for weeks at a time. Without careful monitoring, work issues can easily take the back seat to family issues.

But for most of us, work is more likely the trump card. This is because the impact of letting work slide is generally more immediate and visible than neglecting our family responsibilities. It may take years for the damage done to a family through neglect to be evident, whereas at the office, missing budgets or a bad performance review can show immediately. Hence, the career wheel squeaks more loudly and is likely to get undue attention.

Also, for many of us, it's easier to say no to family than to the boss. And we can rationalize giving priority to work by telling ourselves that when we are working, we're doing so to support our families, so if we put work first, we're doing it for our families. After all, if you don't get that raise, you may tell yourself that you won't be able to buy your daughter the new clothes she wants.

Thus, there's a built-in bias for most of us in favor of work and against our families. Yet the impact from neglecting our families can have just as strong an impact as that from neglecting work. Hence, it would be valuable if we could have family reviews so that the impact of family neglect would be more immediately evident.

When work takes precedence, our relationships suffer; when family takes precedence, our careers suffer. The point of balance is to prevent either work or family from taking precedence, so that neither suffers at the hands of the other. When career and family both get their proper parts in our lives, we've achieved balance.

Illusion: **Balance will create itself.**

Reality: **We must take responsibility to pursue our own balance proactively. We can't wait for someone else, such as our bosses or our spouses, to provide balance for us.**

Establish Boundaries Early On

It's important to establish guidelines or a framework that defines boundaries between work and family.

A job can be like water: It will fill whatever space you give it. This means that you have to restrict the space your job can fill by firmly establishing boundaries between work and home.

Unless you erect borders around work and family, you will be very hard pressed to maintain a balance. Without clear boundaries, you can't determine when one aspect of your life has infringed on the other.

How can we adjust if we can't clearly assess whether our work or family are taking up too many of our resources? We must be consistent in our evaluation and protection of these boundaries so that neither family nor work takes too much of the pie for too much of the time.

Balance is, after all, the ability to have a lot of the things that we want most, most of the time, and if we haven't clearly delineated our different wants, we won't be able to balance them effectively.

One way to build boundaries is to set priorities. Prioritizing is a way of determining what is most important to us. There are two essential components in prioritizing:

1. Knowing how to establish what is most important to us.

2. Knowing what we have to give up. What has to go to the back of the line and wait? (This idea is discussed extensively in Chapter 4.)

Know Your Priorities

We encourage you to take time to understand your priorities. You can easily make a priority list by asking the key question, What do I want?

What do you want? List your top three priorities:

Priority 1: Career (CRP) Build a highly profitable company.

Priority 2: Lexington for family to relax & enjoy & laugh.

Priority 3: Time for family & friends.

Now, list other priorities that also need your attention from time to time.

Other Priorities: *The rest.*

The key to balancing is making choices. We simply have to choose what is most important to us about our family life and work life.

Ask yourself, *What do I need in each part of my life to be happy?*

Select what's important from a career perspective and from a personal perspective. What does your spouse or boyfriend or girlfriend or children, if you have them, think about what is important to you? Do you agree with him or her? Do you think this will change over time?

You should periodically review how your career is going and how your family life is going.

The way to do that is twofold:

First, ask yourself the questions, How is my career going? and How is my family life going?

Second, ask the people in your family (and perhaps others who know you well) the questions, How do you think my career is going? and How do you feel our family life is going?

This isn't easy to do. It requires us to be open to what others say, but in no other way can we be sure that our

20

families or careers are not suffering at the hands of the other (or that one is being achieved at the expense of the other).

There are times in our lives when work takes up more of our time and other times when family or personal issues dominate our time. For example, when there is a birth or a death in the family, work issues tend to be set aside. Or when there is a crisis at work, family matters tend to get sidelined.

But we must recognize that at these moments, events have driven our lives out of balance, and we must look for or create an opportunity to reallocate our time and energy.

It can be difficult to determine our priorities. In this decision-making process, people who don't share our values or priorities and don't have much of a stake in our lives can be a real danger. They may try to impose expectations, demands, or activities on us, presenting them as moral or social obligations, which we then feel obliged to meet in addition to our careers and our families.

Other-imposed "obligations" might include social events that we just have to attend because friends insist, community service opportunities that would be nice to do, and volunteer church and charity activities that become onerous. In balance, such activities add interest and variety to our lives; out of balance, they can add dead weight.

Many things would be fun or nice to do, but the time for them must often come out of the time that we would otherwise devote to family or career—and there can be too little time left for these top-priority things. The good, the things that would be fun or nice to do, become enemies of the best—our families and careers.

Obviously, too much outside activity reduces our time and perhaps our devotion for career and family, leaving us with a tough tradeoff: We are forced to choose between career and family in the time that remains to us. This choice may destroy our efforts to balance career and family.

Be satisfied with your choices. Make a few big decisions about what you want in life and stick with them, at least for a designated period of time.

One of the biggest mistakes we can make is constantly to doubt the choices we've made in setting our priorities. We must simply come to terms with our choices and be satisfied with our decisions . . . until we reach a point of serious reevaluation.

We suggest that you schedule an annual reevaluation session (discussed in Chapter 6) and that you don't second-guess yourself until your designated session.

An Exercise in Perspective

Our perspective can influence our ability to be satisfied with our choices.

Imagine for a moment that you are looking at a glass of water. Some people will look at the glass and see it as being half full; others will see the glass as half empty. It's all a matter of perspective.

 Do you see the glass as half empty or half full?

The truth is this:

You can emphasize what is lacking or highlight what is there, and your perspective will influence your capacity to be happy with your priorities. Do you see your work, marriage, or family life as half empty or half full? Do you emphasize what is lacking or highlight what is there? Changing your perspective can influence your capacity to be happy with your priorities and your choices.

By making decisions about what is important to you and not second-guessing those decisions daily, you can then be more engaged and happier with your choices. Also, by understanding your priorities, you can reduce the guilt and anxiety associated with trying to meet work and family wants and needs.

Define Success on Your Own Terms

Our concept of *how much is enough* can change as our wealth increases. The more we begin associating with others who have greater means, the more our eyes open to the possibilities of what "more" can do. As we compare our outcomes with others around us, we engage in a never-ending cycle of wanting more. What we have—and even who we are—then are never enough.

When we fall into a comparison mode, we are using external benchmarks for our success, and although this seems logical when competing with colleagues or neighbors, this can be a major obstacle in defining and creating our own balance.

External benchmarks

- Other people's career success
- Other people's income or position
- Other people's house, car, or vacation
- Other people's wealth, asset, or acquisition
- Other people's parties, clubs, or opportunities

Internal benchmarks

- Our feelings about ourselves
- Our family's feelings about themselves

24

Step 2

5/29/04

- Our contributions to others

- Our own growth, improvement, and progress

Leaders are especially vulnerable to this comparison cycle as they climb the professional ladder. What seemed like enough a year or two ago suddenly seems insufficient for each new position. The higher we climb, the greater the views; the more we put into the system, the more that comes out. And the more we have, the more we may want.

The theme of *higher, faster, further* results in *more and more and more* expectations—and these may not be healthy or wise for us.

Define balance on your own terms, using internal benchmarks to stop this comparison cycle—know when enough is truly enough. There will always be people with more than you and people with less than you.

Critical Success Factors in Balancing What Is Most Important to You

In balancing what you want, here are some critical success factors:

- Create balance: It will not emerge without effort, and it cannot simply be stumbled upon.

- Establish boundaries between your working and family environments to achieve balance.

- Stick by your decisions. Once you've made your choices, you must be satisfied with them. This decreases the guilt and anxiety that results from second-guessing yourself.

- Define success on your own terms. Benchmarking your success externally results in a never-ending cycle in which the more you see, the more you want. Balance frees you to be happy with what you have.

Make Choices and Accept the Consequences: *Giving Up What You Don't Want Badly Enough*

You now need to make some tough choices, because balance is achieved by letting go of those things that you don't want as much. These lower-level matters may masquerade as first-tier priorities, but you can tell what matters most when you have to let go of something.

Once we have identified the things in work and family that we want most, we next need to identify what we don't want as much. The art of balancing our career and family involves limiting the number of tradeoffs between them, which allows us to do both as much as possible.

*Everything comes with a price—
even achieving balance.*

Balance is about getting as much of our family and career as we can. The way we achieve this is by eliminating the things that trick us into thinking they are top priorities when they aren't.

Just Let It Go

We achieve balance by understanding what things we are willing to put on the back burner—the things that we are willing to let go of so that we can make room for those things that we *do* want most.

I will let go of...

- People who pretend to be my friends and take my time
- Things that would be nice to do but aren't really important to do
- Meaningless activities that don't create anything and that don't refresh me for more important things
- Trivial gossip, TV shows, and time wasters

To make room for...

- Quality time with my family

- Time to focus on my work

- Time for refreshing myself

- Exercise to keep me healthy

- Time to help my spouse and children (or my parents or siblings or boy- or girlfriend) with their projects and needs

The art of balancing is to get involved as much as we can with our family and career without giving up one for the other.

First Tier or Second Tier?

We also have many wants and desires that aren't "first things" (top priorities) that we should put second or perhaps even clear off the calendar altogether.

Our ability to differentiate first-tier priorities from lower-priority items will boost our success at balancing our career and family wants. These "first-tier" priorities might shift with the seasons, so we encourage you to identify your top priorities now.

For example, as the authors of this book, we offer our own first-tier priorities (at our respective stages):

Quinn Mills

- Finish key projects

- Start a second career

- Help my children finish college

- Help my children launch their careers

Kirstin Hornby

- Graduate from Harvard Business School with my MBA degree

- Start my career

- Make time for a serious relationship

- Start a family

Sasha Mattu

- Get reacquainted with my brothers and sisters (I've been out of the country a long time)

- Decide in what direction to pursue my career

■ Enjoy my life as a single woman for a while longer—take time for myself

■ Meet people who support me in my goals and make friendships with them

When we give up things that are not really as important to us to have more of those things that are, we are clearing the decks, making room for what is truly important to us. Those things that we can't call priorities must go to the back of the line (or out of the line if they no longer have a place in our lives).

Know Your Limits

We all have natural limits. We are limited to different degrees in talent, ambition, patience, intelligence, and qualities such as resilience, discipline, skill, empathy, endurance, knowledge, and experience. Certain limits appear to be common to us all in much the same way, including the limitations of time and attention span, concentration, focus, and energy.

Time

We have a finite number of hours in the day and only so many years in our lives; we can't possibly have everything all at once, all of the time. Time is our most scarce resource, and it can be easily misallocated.

The temptation for those of us who are driven to succeed is incrementally to dedicate more and more time to our professional efforts to "stay ahead of the pack." In fact, that is often the expectation.

In business, we may think that we will be outdone by individuals who allocate more time to professional success. If measured in short-term success, this may be the case. However, we believe that over time, balance between work and family facilitates success in both domains.

But time is not our only limitation.

Attention Span, Concentration, Focus, and Energy

These resources are also important and, like time, are limited. If we are trying to do too much, we become spread too thin, and the degree to which we can focus decreases.

Thus, time management, along with the ability to prioritize between first- and second-tier priorities (life leadership), is a vital skill—and one that can be learned and improved with practice and with the consistent application of proven time and life management principles.

If this area is a challenge for you, as it is for many professionals, we suggest that you seek the specialized training or tools (planners and organizers) to strengthen your competence in resource management.

Step 3

Minimize Tradeoffs

If you have two highly prized possessions, perhaps your home and your new car, would you want to trade one for the other? Of course not. And yet . . .

We make tradeoffs in life and at work when...

We give up something that is very important to us to get something else that is of equal or greater importance to us.

These choices are particularly difficult because they are between first-tier priorities. We understand that in balancing those things that we want most, tradeoffs are often necessary. (If this weren't the case, we wouldn't be writing a book on how to balance career and family.)

But many of us have an exaggerated view of how many tradeoffs are necessary in order to be balanced. We tend to think that many of the choices we make involve tradeoffs when they really don't. This is because people often confuse less important items—second-tier items— with more important first-tier items.

In balance, we minimize the number of tradeoffs we need to make because we have a clear idea of what rates as a first-tier priority and what might be considered less essential at the time.

We need to identify nonessential items and clear the deck of them so we can tell when we are choosing between top-priority items—and make as few of these tradeoffs as possible.

At Harvard University, for example, we often witness amazing stories of people who, at least for a few years of focused study, decide that many things in life are less important than successfully completing their chosen programs. For a season of their lives, some students try to get along without many comforts (doing without everything from long baths to a full night's sleep) and conveniences (doing without everything from cars to cell phones) and clear the deck of all nonessentials. At the worst extreme, the discarded items may include friends and family ties, along with basic hygiene and health maintenance.

On a positive note, many university students learn the power of focus and concentration. They learn that they can be happy and fulfilled without many material comforts. Indeed, many learn which people, places, and things should take priority in their lives. And, having learned those lessons, they are better able to minimize the need to make tradeoffs among first-tier priorities.

A tradeoff means making choices between our top priorities.

The art to having life-work balance is not to become good or wise at making tradeoffs, but rather to minimize the number of tradeoffs we make.

A tradeoff is always, by our definition, a win–lose situation because it occurs between those things we want most. Many of our balancing decisions are actually between something that we want more (a first-tier item) and something else that we want less (a second-tier item); this is not tradeoff.

The more specific our priorities are, the fewer the tradeoffs we are forced to make. In this way, we may give-up something, but we also gain a lot—a balance between career and family—which reduces both current tension and future regret.

Blind Tradeoffs

Sometimes we aren't aware of the tradeoffs that we are making as a result of our choices. This is why we emphasize the importance of taking responsibility and proactively creating our own balance. In this way, we can minimize having to make tradeoffs with our eyes closed.

For example, we may be blind to the following tradeoffs:

- If we choose to take a new job with lots of travel, we trade off time with our family.

- If we join a new club, we may trade off time to spend on work or family.

- If we tie up an evening with a new TV series, we trade off helping our children with their school homework or personal projects.

Marielle, a lawyer in Boston, reminds us to be wary of making choices that force us into unnecessary tradeoffs simply because we're confused about which things are and aren't important. Her story highlights the blind choices we might make when trying to balance a family and career, resulting in long-term tradeoffs that we later regret.

MARIELLE'S STORY

Honestly, I don't think a balance between work and family in the short term is possible—at least not for me as a lawyer, trying to make partner in my firm. It seems like I would have to sacrifice either one thing or the other—either stepping off the fast track at work or losing touch with my family—if I tried to do both.

My plan is simple. I'm going to work hard for several years at the start of my career, get well established and successful, make some money, then have a family. By the time I have my family, the most time-consuming part of my career will be over, and I'll have lots of time for my children and my husband. I thought about trying to have a family now. I could marry my boyfriend, assuming he's willing, which I think he is, and have a child, and I'd really like to do it, but you know how things go.

Even if I could devote the same amount of time to my job as I do now, simply taking a few weeks off for maternity leave would be seen as a strike against me. Suddenly, I am no longer an equal to my peers, but instead a "Mom." I wouldn't be taken as seriously; I'd be put in a special category and people would say, even though they were just trying to be kind, "Maybe we shouldn't involve her in this project because it'll take her away from her baby," and I'll fall right off the advancement ladder— without many people even realizing it. I'm not going to let that happen to my career. I'll stay with it until I make it to the top, and I should still have time to have a family.

The Risk of Either–Or Thinking

Marielle's plan is an attractive strategy because it promises that we can have it all—a full career, *then* a fulfilling relationship with our family. But the risks of failure with this strategy are high. What if being a success in your career takes too long and you don't ever get around to having a family? What if you have a family while you're focused on your career, then discover that you've short-changed your family and yourself because of your career?

Often, these high-risk strategies result from either–or thinking that creates false dichotomies (thinking that you can have either this . . . or that . . . but not both). For example:

- I can have either a chance to get ahead in my career or a marriage.

- I can either have a baby or have a career.

- I can either pursue my dreams or keep this job.

Opposite Illusions

In the end, it's an illusion that we can easily compartmentalize our lives, that we can devote the first 10 or 20 years to our careers and the remainder to our family. It's too great a risk, and we'll end up with too many regrets for what we've missed.

Illusion: **We can fulfill our career goals and our family goals at separate times during our lives.**

Reality: **Balance is achieved by pursuing both a career and family simultaneously. If we sacrifice our career goals to satisfy our family goals, we are not balanced. If we focus on our career at the expense of our families, we are not balanced.**

Many of us believe we can achieve balance over our lifetime by being focused *first* on our career, *then* on our family. But the trouble is that once we finally decide to shift our focus to our family, it may be too late; they may have already grown up or, for some, they never even got started. Thinking "first this" and "then that" may lead to tradeoffs between first-tier priorities.

We must ask ourselves the question, How long do we realistically think it will be before we can start our family if we choose to invest in our career first?

Having It All...and Making It Work

In Marielle's case, it may be three more years before she makes partner. Of course, there is competition in her workplace that also needs to be accounted for.

An additional consideration for Marielle (and many other women in her shoes) is whether to be concerned about becoming too old to have children. Many women believe that with the advances in medicine, they can have children into their mid-40s, making it reasonable to focus on putting a career in order by age 35, finding someone to want to be with by age 37, and having children between the ages of 38 and 45. This is not a rule of thumb that's proven or reliable. Some women find comfort in knowing that there is always the option of adopting, if need be.

But even if women were able to find the right man at the right time and to fit in having children, wouldn't it still be difficult simply to leave a career that has been developing for years to start a family? In fact, as we saw with Marielle, as a partner in her firm, won't the time demands become even greater? Certainly, the responsibilities and pressures will be. And with the record for long hours she has established at the workplace, would she suddenly be able to adjust her work to have time for a family? Probably not.

This situation might not be more conducive to raising a family than her current situation, and she would still require a lot of support from a spouse or someone else in her life. Finding a spouse who can provide that level of help won't be easy, especially if she's giving herself a one- or two-year window to find him. And with the hours she would need to put into becoming a leader in her career, how much time would she have for dating? This strategy isn't feasible.

It might be made easier for her if her spouse takes a responsible approach to fatherhood. Men sometimes approach the issue of work and family in a less responsible way than do many women. Men will often become fathers without intending to devote the amount of time necessary to raising children well. Instead, they plan to leave child rearing to the mother, even if it means that the mother is either overwhelmed by tasks that need to be done or must give up her career. A responsible man recognizes that a child or children will need him, not just the mother, and will plan the future of his career to provide time for family as well as work—that is, to attain balance.

But it remains an illusion that a person can first do one thing, then the other, in sequence in their lives, and derive a kind of balance over time between work and family. People who try this strategy almost never achieve a real balance in their lives—instead, they are first unbalanced one way, then the other.

The opposite approach doesn't work either—the notion that we can put family first, then try to go back later in life to build a successful career. This strategy ordinarily fails because it's usually too late to get onto the career path. There are too many leaders who have tried this and failed. They've worked a few years, then left their jobs to have families and spent years raising their kids, then tried to return to the business world. Most of them have new jobs, but they aren't on a career ladder and certainly aren't achieving the career goals they once had. They look back at what they had and wish they could recapture career momentum.

Illusion: **We can make up later in life for what we've put aside earlier.**

Reality: **We can't make up later in life for what we've put aside earlier. If we focus on our careers at the expense of our families, we'll miss our children growing up, and we'll never get that back. Conversely, if we drop off the career track to raise families, it's almost impossible to get back on, and we'll miss the opportunity to achieve our career goals.**

We can't recapture the youth of our children if we sacrifice them to our careers, and we can't recapture our place on the promotion ladder if we sacrifice it to our children. To believe that we can set something aside now and regain it years later is an illusion. We can't recapture the years of a child's life that we sacrifice to friends and diversions; we can't recapture the opportunities for lifelong relationships that we miss because we're too busy doing other things; we can't recapture our position on a promotion ladder because we were distracted elsewhere.

Say No

Even when making tradeoffs consciously, it isn't always easy. As leaders, we tend to take on more than we can handle, which can hinder our ability to be balanced. The ability to say no to outside obligations is a skill that we need to develop.

At different times and seasons of your life, you may need to say no to such "obligations" as:

- offices in clubs or community organizations
- church offices or charity work
- committee assignments at work
- responsibilities for elaborate celebrations

We know how difficult it can be to say no outside of the home. It requires courage to say it and the perspective to realize that one small commitment can crowd out some of the most important things in our lives.

Committing to...	Can crowd out...
A new car	A new house
A new baby	A new job
A new job	An advanced degree

There is a degree to which being "outcome-oriented" about life is helpful, but should we become too focused, everything else can go out of focus. The key to maintaining a happy life is being able to say no when necessary—and not feeling guilty about those things we can't manage.

Don't Feel Guilty

We can't afford to feel guilty about the things we can't control or manage. We must distinguish between things that are in our control and things that are not.

Step 3

Things we can control	Things we can't control
What jobs we accept	The job requirements
How we spend our time	What our boss assigns us to outside work
The commitments we take	The needs of our spouse, family/friends or our children/grandchildren

Of course, we can't attribute success only to our own personal choices. We often limit the causes of our happiness by our own management of a situation. In psychology, we call this "the fundamental attribution error." We attribute the outcome of a situation, whether positive or negative, solely to an individual rather than to the outside situation itself.

This can make it more difficult for leaders to say no to those things that they don't want badly enough because they see this choice stemming from a short-coming within themselves. It's as though not being able to do it all somehow reflects on a leader's core self as being inadequate. This is not the case.

We must remember:

A **successful balance** means attaining **many** of those things that are **most** important to us.

This means being free to say no without guilt and to let those things go that we can't manage.

Nathan owns his own retail business and discusses how he learned this skill.

NATHAN'S STORY

I don't think I'm a magician or anything special. It really came down to being honest with myself about what I wanted out of my life, what's going to work for me, and ignoring all the loud noises outside that told me what I should be doing. I knew that I may have to make these decisions for myself and that I would have to be comfortable with these decisions once I made them.

I was aware that whatever decisions I made, I would have to make a few tradeoffs. I can't have it all, all the time. If I say that family will always take the highest priority, the likely outcome is that I will make certain decisions that will not be in complete support of my career and that has to be okay with me, in my very heart. I can't let anyone on the outside make me feel bad about that. If they are able to make me feel bad, then maybe I haven't really decided. But if I can make informed decisions and be flexible and comfortable with my decisions, I think it is possible for almost anyone.

Why It's Hard to Say No

Nathan reminds us that the guilt and difficulty in saying no can partly be attributed to external pressures. This could be from our spouse, children, supervisors, or co-workers. In the realm of family and in the realm of work, we need to be able to manage the expectations of others. Saying no is simply one step.

Nathan also emphasizes the importance of knowing our own priorities because there will be many loud and competing objectives in our lives—among them, parental voices, social values, professional opportunity, and job relocation.

The key to being balanced is to know what is most important and what isn't while we move toward creating our own balance.

Critical Success Factors in Giving Up What You Don't Want Badly Enough

- Balance is about getting as much of your family and career wants as you can. This means you must minimize the tradeoffs between them.

- Tradeoffs are always a win–lose situation because you have to choose between your first priorities.

■ Choose between those things you want most and those things that aren't as important.

■ Clear the decks of second-tier items to make room for those things that you want most.

■ Let go of the things you don't want badly enough and minimize guilt when you have to say no.

■ If you don't clearly know what is most important to you, you'll likely make unnecessary and regretful tradeoffs.

Choose a Career that Supports Balance: *Making Your Balance Real*

First you need to be smart about your career choices because some careers are much more conducive to work–life balance than others. And once you are working within your chosen career, you need to safeguard balance by making wise moves, creating a path that is uniquely yours. Although the basic options—staying with the organization, moving laterally, or leaving—remain constant, you can gain the flexibility you need to succeed.

Having It All...and Making It Work

How we choose to balance our career and family has many implications. In this chapter, we focus on what implications and challenges we face in our careers and how to ensure that our career choices are helping and not hindering our ability to achieve balance. By making wise career choices, we make our balance real.

Your environment shouldn't stifle balance—it should promote it.

We have discussed the balance framework: what it is and how to get it. The next two chapters take our process to another level. This chapter focuses on career tips, what things we can do to identify and shape our careers to facilitate and nurture our balancing choices. Chapter 5 delves into how we can manage our family domain to strengthen our long-term commitment and capacity for balance. And in Chapter 6, we discuss how to regain balance when you are off and how to keep in balance most of the time.

Balancing our families with our careers may require making choices between happiness and ambition. Happiness is generally associated with achieving personal goals and a successful family life; career satisfaction is the result of achieving our professional ambitions for our careers. Sometimes there are tradeoffs between these things—success in our careers takes such time from our families that we must sacrifice some happiness, or success in our family life causes us to sacrifice career success.

Balancing career and family will test our ability to be successful in both career and family, because many of us think that we can find happiness by *first* driving hard and succeeding in the career domain, *then* attending to family. But as we age and gain experience, career achievements seem less likely to provide real happiness than success in our personal lives.

Choose Your Career Path Wisely

Balancing will therefore require us to choose our professions carefully. Certain professions (such as investment banking, due to the long hours, or consulting, due to the travel) do not allow for balance. It will also require us to select positions within our chosen profession carefully, because certain positions will be better suited to our life balance needs than others. But almost any job or career choice will present challenges, because working requires a major commitment of time and energy.

We also need to be proactive in *seeking* and *shaping* organizations that are more amenable to accepting our priorities.

Seek: *Fortune*'s "best companies to work for." If you're a woman, seek the most women-friendly companies. If you're a minority, seek organizations that promote diversity. In other words, seek organizations that are known to be family-friendly or that represent the "best fit" for you at your age and stage of life.

Shape: Any company you now work for. Help shape its policies and practices. Influence its mission and direction. Shape its culture, or at least the culture of your team, group, or division.

Job Match and Balancing Act

Seek out careers in which balancing actions are possible. Not all jobs and career options lend themselves to work–life balance. Some work situations make our ability to balance a career and family more difficult.

If you are already firmly entrenched in a career path, decide how long you will remain in that path, whether to attempt to change the work culture toward greater commitment flexibility, or whether to find a better-balanced work opportunity.

Certain careers and companies are simply less flexible and tolerant of balance than others, so you need to enter with your eyes wide open; otherwise, you may later feel trapped, confronted with tradeoffs, or compromised in your commitments.

Illusion: I can choose whatever job or career I like best without regard to my family, then I can somehow find time for my family too.

Reality: We have to choose our jobs and careers carefully to be sure they permit us to have enough time for our families.

Three Fundamental Options

When making your balancing decisions whether choosing a new path or continuing a pre-existing career, you face three fundamental choices:

■ **Option 1: *Stay at your current job.*** This may mean, however, that you must take initiative and be pro-active, not passive, about changing corporate culture to support your need for balance.

■ **Option 2: *Move laterally within the company.*** If you can't change the culture of your current job but you like where you are, we suggest moving laterally within the same organization.

■ **Option 3:** *Leave the company.* If all else fails—leave. Find a career or new position that allows you to have a lot of those things you want most in life and at work.

Capable professionals will always have options. Even in a tight job market or recession economy, you can either find or create options that are more compatible with your family and career objectives.

Six Ways to Create Space

By "space," we mean creating the feeling that you are not captive, at the mercy of the organization or the market. If you choose Option 1 and decide to stay at your current workplace and manage the culture (or at least the culture of your team), you can create and maintain the space you need for balance in six ways:

1. Experiment
2. Become irreplaceable
3. Trust and delegate
4. Spread the word
5. Minimize stress
6. Protect your weekend time

Let's discuss each of these strategies.

Step 4

1. Experiment. Try to be creative with your manager. For a short time, show that increased flexibility will not hamper your productivity. Most managers fear that if they allow you the flexibility to balance family with work, you will become less productive. So set up a time period in which you can show how balance makes you better at both!

Jane describes the experimental phase she created with her boss to achieve the balance that she wanted.

JANE'S STORY

I felt like I was always battling against the firm's culture, especially as a young mother, trying to find time to raise my children. One day, I sat down with my boss and had a very frank conversation with him. I told him that my performance was suffering because of the constant conflict I was feeling. My schedule was simply too rigid for me to get to see enough of my children. He agreed to give me a chance for one month and during that month he gave me all the flexibility I needed. I worked very hard that month to prove to him that flexibility would help me in my work for the company and not hinder others or me. My productivity went up; I made fewer errors; and was generally happier, which had a positive impact on our customers, people who reported to me, and even my boss. My boss recognized how effective the experiment had been, and soon others were trying it, too. I learned a couple of very important lessons in that time: The key to any larger change in attitude in the company is to talk to other people who work there about making the company more family-friendly.

You need to take responsibility. It's your life. The company might not be looking out for you, but that means you have to look out for yourself. Talk to your manager—state your needs. Help your company to understand that balanced, healthy people make better employees. Prove that to your managers. It's too easy to get caught up in the rat race and forget about the rest of your life. You have a lot more control over your time than you might imagine. Reprioritize. Leave for your kids' soccer games early, and kick that report out of the water that weekend, or even get it in early. If we are living satisfying lives, we perform better, more quickly, and smarter. We're more productive, while those who are guilt-ridden will be less so. It is our responsibility to teach these lessons to our bosses and peers.

2. Become irreplaceable. Carve out a niche so that you become irreplaceable. This will give you leveraging power to negotiate your position. Unique skills come with power over colleagues, clients, and even competitors—it's the power to say, "I will do it tomorrow." This may not be possible, however, in all careers.

There are a number of ways to make yourself irreplaceable: Be the only person in your office to know key things about the business and its customers; have skills that are crucial to others' work but that they lack; have a special relationship with key customers or suppliers. The notion that a person becomes irreplaceable by being the hardest worker is often wrong, and people who try this route are disappointed. Hard work will make you valuable and may get you promoted; it will not make you irreplaceable in your current position.

3. Trust and delegate. If we truly want to restrict our jobs from intruding on all aspect of our lives, we need to learn to delegate. Delegation requires the self-awareness of leaders who can candidly admit that some people are better at—or have more time for—some things than they do. It takes courage to delegate responsibility, but it's worth it in the long term if it means more room to focus on other, more important things in your life.

This also means that we have to learn to trust others. We must trust our co-workers before we are able to delegate more power to them. Without the ability to trust and delegate, we can't accomplish the tasks required of us or find ourselves at home with our families at reasonable times. Learning this skill will greatly improve our capacity to be leaders.

Jenny found that once she started delegating, she was able to create the necessary space to help her create balance.

JENNY'S STORY

After debating with my husband, I realized that I simply have too many responsibilities at work and had to ask my boss if I could transfer one of my projects to a colleague. This was difficult because I prided myself with the attitude of being able to take on anything that was thrown my way. But I realized I could not be a balanced leader and also do everything, so I decided to give it a shot. My husband also agreed to decrease his amount of travel. This meant spending extra time training his employees to do this for him, but in the long run, less travel greatly loosened up his schedule and ability to be there for the family.

Jenny and her husband both had to learn to trust others and delegate to create more space for each other.

4. Spread the word. Talk to others around you at work and at home about your lifestyle. Get the word out. Today, many people—mostly women—drop out of the work force early, including those who have spent a lot of money on formal education and who had, at one point, the desire to succeed in their careers.

Today, many women with professional degrees don't have professional careers! Some may not have careers because they want to spend almost all their time with their families, but more do it because they don't think balance is possible. They think they have to give up their families to have a career, yet for most of them, balance is possible.

The more we spread the word among working professionals that balance is possible, the more accepted this fact will become. More people will stay in the work force, and fewer people will be frustrated because they don't have a career or because they are working too much and spending too little time with their children.

We also have to let people at work know about what we're doing in our private lives—at least we have to if we expect them to be understanding and sympathetic. How can we expect our bosses or co-workers to be supportive of us when we have to leave work early or skip a day and leave them with extra work, if we haven't told them why?

Having It All...and Making It Work

There are many ways to let others into our lives. If we have children, let others know this with small, short, verbal mentions each day. Let them know of successes and failures, of aspirations and achievements in sports, school, or other activities. Over time, people will become familiar with your family; and if you need help at some time, they are more likely to provide it. Bringing the idea of family into the workplace through company events, pictures, or conversation helps to soften the whole culture to the idea of family. Remember, of course, not to be offensive with this approach. Disrupting work by spending too much time on your own interests and those of your family can become tiresome. Even here, getting the balance correct is crucial.

In general, we get help when we need it because we've prepared the way—because we've let others learn about us and others in our lives so that they are interested, involved, and sympathetic. We get help when we need it because we deserve it, and we haven't sprung our need unexpectedly on people. Thinking ahead and preparing the way when we don't have an immediate need is about creating positive relationships with others, not simply trying to lean on them when we need something.

If we want people to be supportive, we have to let them be on our team, and that means we have to let them in. We also need to be aware of others' family needs. Some people with whom we share our balance may not understand, but the more we share, the more we will begin surrounding ourselves with like-minded people, which will add to our support structure and make balancing that much easier.

5. Minimize stress. Managing the work environment can be difficult, and it's important to find a healthy way to deal with the stress. There are many effective ways to cope with the pressures at work:

- Be organized, plan in advance how to handle likely difficulties.

- Prioritize work issues so that the most stressful get handled first.

- Delegate to others matters they can handle.

- Mentor others in handling what are for you especially stressful matters.

To cope with stress at home, you might try exercising, watching a movie, reading a good novel, coaching a team, or volunteering your service. Where young children are present, it's very important for parents or grandparents to spell each other in handling the cares and concerns presented by children.

We must develop our own unique combination of activities that helps alleviate any additional tension.

6.Protect your weekend time. Again, we encourage you to set clear boundaries between work and home and to manage these boundaries proactively to protect your private time at home in the evening and on the weekend.

For example, because no one at work is going to suggest to us that we take time off to take care of our children, we need to take responsibility for delivering on our promises to our families. This may mean establishing credibility early that reduced hours do not mean reduced output or communicating our needs (e.g., "I leave work by 6:00 P.M. every day") to fellow workers and sticking by them, while ensuring that our jobs get done.

You *can* help manage culture. You can set the tone at work for a supportive community that provides the flexibility to find your own balance. In a time when two-career families are trying to have it all with less community support, you and your family have to do more on your own.

In many careers, we aren't judged by the number of hours we work but by how well we live up to our commitments. At work, we should strive not only to create the structures to support a family-friendly environment but also to build a community to support these structures.

This may seem a tall order—that a person can achieve career success by arranging with her or his employer a situation more supportive of family life. In fact, a single person may not be able to do it, but a group of people supporting one another may well make significant progress in this direction.

Step to the Side

Now, suppose that you have tried our six steps (summarized at the end of the book) to create space and influence the culture of your company. You're in a company that you like, but the culture is resistant to any changes that would help you achieve balance. You wish you could get a promotion and still have more opportunity for balancing family and career, but that may not be possible.

So what do you do now? Select Option 2—move laterally. Get somewhere else in the company and see whether that position works better for you.

Sometimes you may need to leave a company, but often you can simply change jobs to create a situation where balance is more feasible.

Many professionals tend to look down on lateral movements. They think of horizontal movement as a career killer. The notion is that if a person makes a lateral move, it's because he or she cannot get a promotion from his or her current job, and this suggests that the person doesn't merit a promotion. So the argument is that it's best to stay in your current job and wait for a promotion. But in reality, that's simply not the case.

Some very effective people have built stellar careers using a lot of lateral moves. For example, Lewis Gerstner, former CEO of IBM, moved from a consulting company to financial services company, to a foods company, to a high-tech manufacturer, advancing his career at each step. He climbed no ladder in a single company but moved among them, advancing his career at each move.

It's fine to use lateral movement to try to find balance. It's an effective way to negotiate a balance between our career and family wants while decreasing the stress from a job that is making us unbalanced.

Many leaders struggle with a tunnel vision approach when pursuing career advancement. They look for the quickest way from point A to point B. But in reality, we can still get from point A to B, perhaps even in a way that allows us to get more of the things that we really want along the way.

By using your imagination, you can find solutions to meet both your personal and career needs. The lateral move strategy can be a lifesaver at times.

Are You Climbing a Career Ladder or Lattice?

Most people think of careers as climbing up a ladder when, in reality, we should see our careers as a lattice — a combination of many ladders next to one another and connected.

Step 4

Let's suppose we are at rung number 3 (represented by the O) and trying to climb to rung 4 on the way to the top at rung 9. But suppose there's someone in the job at rung 4 who's not moving, and so we are blocked at rung 4 (see the X on rung 4 in the diagram). In this case, most people think that we have only two options—to stay on rung 3 indefinitely until rung 4 opens up or to leave the firm.

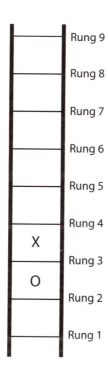

But why not take a different approach? Below is a diagram of a promotion lattice. Every firm, except the very smallest, is like this—that is, it has more than one department and each department has a promotion ladder. We can climb the lattice either by going up rung by rung or by going sideways and *then* up rung by rung. For example, rather than staying in a job that is in one of the ladders, and in which you're blocked from going higher, you make a lateral move to a job on another ladder, where there's not a block above you, and then

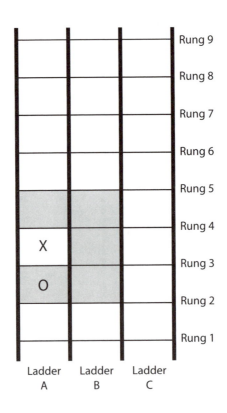

move up that ladder. Over time, when you're successful in the new department, you might even move back to the old department at a higher job level than the one that you left. The point is to be flexible and keep a good attitude, so that people think well of you. Never burn a bridge by leaving a department or a firm in a huff, just because you're blocked from promotion at a certain time. Instead, look for other opportunities, be pleasant, and maybe you'll even return some day. In our chart opposite this means that you might move laterally from Ladder A (where you are blocked from promotion to Rung 4) to Ladder B at Rung 3, then up Ladder B to Rung 4, and maybe back to Ladder A at Rung 5.

How long should we stay in a job (on a rung) to see whether what appears to be a block above really is? Should we wait one year; or two, or five, or ten? The answer is about eighteen months to two years. If you are a person with leadership talent, you should be moving up the ladder every eighteen months to two years; if you are not moving up that frequently, you should think about moving laterally to get on a ladder that gives you more upside potential.

Opt Out

Let's look at yet a different situation. Suppose that you've now tried to implement the six tips to changing the culture of your current employment, and you've also tried to move laterally, but this has not worked. What do you do now?

Get the heck out of there! If you can't change the culture, and this culture prevents you from being balanced, you should leave because the consequences of staying are worse. You'll give up too much because you can't have enough of the things that are important to you, and this can only end in bad tradeoffs and bitter regret.

Four Key Career Levers

As you search for work that promotes balance, you might review your most important priorities and use four key levers—travel, vacation time, commuting time, and responsibility within job—to determine whether a new job prospect will help or hinder your efforts for greater balance.

You might consider each of these four factors when selecting a job or thinking about a promotion. These will either help or hurt your ability to balance a career and family. Decide how much of each you can have and still balance your life. When you've made the decision, find a job and a place to live that correspond with what you've decided.

Step 4

1. **Agree on travel needs.** Consider the amount of work travel necessary for your job and agree beforehand with your boss how much traveling each month you are willing and able to do. In your previous job, were you away from home at least half of the nights of the year? Was this a tremendous strain on your family? Did you miss many of your kids' most important events? Depending on how you answer these questions, you will want to negotiate travel demands in your next employment situation.

2. **Take vacation time!** Don't wait for a perfect time to do so—the perfect time for a vacation will never come. Deciding to actually take vacations, all of them, can be a big change in itself. Wouldn't it make a difference to spend a full two weeks with your family, leaving your cell phone off, and your laptop at home? Although it may initially be a difficult transition, you will be surprised at how rejuvenated you feel when you return from vacation to work.

3. **Limit the commuting time between work and home.** Consider the location of a new job. Have you been previously working in the city while living in a suburb, resulting in at least two hours of commuting a day? A solution to this is to find an office closer to home or to chose a city with an easy

69

commute. The choice of location is very critical to balance, because it makes a tremendous difference to have an extra hour or two per day to devote to family or work. It means that your family may have to sacrifice a little in terms of the location of your home or the city you want to live in, or one parent may have to choose a different job—but this is what it takes to find balance.

4. **Limit responsibility.** Take only as much responsibility within your job as you can handle without becoming a slave to your work. Carefully consider the level of responsibility you will willingly accept. This can be the most difficult lever for people who are accustomed to wanting and having full control. But to accept too much responsibility at work and still expect to go home regularly by 6:00 P.M. is a recipe for disaster. So when looking at new companies, go in knowing that you will have to put some limitations on how much time you will devote to your career. Over the course of a career, you may need to say no to additional responsibility and to more money, as well. But at other times, as your children grow into their own lives, you may be able to accept more responsibility. It's more a matter of timing than a final, ultimate choice.

Choose a career that is fulfilling, rather than one that only provides an outcome (e.g., "I need to make X million dollars in five years, then retire"). Trading off the present for grand retirement schemes rarely works.

If you enjoy what you do at work and continue to develop personally, you will in turn be able to be a better father/mother or partner. Your career choices should help, not hinder, your balancing choices.

Critical Success Factors in Making Your Balance Real

- Not all careers promote the possibility for balance: Choose careers in which balancing actions are possible.

- If you don't have balance in your current work situation, you can change the culture of your current job, move laterally within the organization, or if all else fails, leave.

- You can manage the culture of our workplace by proactively taking action that involves your bosses and colleagues.

- Lateral movement can be a good tool to achieve balance in your current working environment.

■ Don't be afraid to leave your current employment if you aren't given the space to create balance; otherwise, you risk ending up with regrets for all the things you've missed.

■ When making a new career decision, take into account the major aspects that influence your ability to balance—and choose wisely.

STEP 5

Involve Your Loved Ones in Creating Balance: *Refining Your Balance*

You can't create balance in a vacuum. When you involve your significant others at home and at work in designing and refining your work-family balance plan, you will have greater success. It is especially important to have both parents in balance.

In the previous few chapters, we discussed how we can understand, define, and prioritize those things that are most important to us in our career and families, then provided ways to engage in dialogue with bosses and co-workers. This process also applies to family matters. Refining our balance always means giving due time and attention to friends and family.

Four Strategies

We can strengthen our long-term capacity for balance by better managing the family domain. We invite you to try these four tips:

1. Involve all team members.
2. Understand family concerns.
3. Be creative in the way we spend time with our kids.
4. Make sure that both parents have a chance to have balanced lives.

Again, let's discuss each of these strategies for achieving family balance.

1. Involve All Our Team Members When Creating Our Balance

Family members and significant others need to be involved in determining our long-term, sustainable life plan since it requires an understanding of the priorities of family members along with their "buy-in" to our balancing decisions. A colleague once shared this story with us:

I was once offered a year's stay at a great university in England. It would have opened a whole new set of acquaintances and career opportunities for me. I spoke to my wife about it. She asked, "What will I be doing?"

"What do you mean?" I asked.

"I see why this would be a great career move for you. But what about me? I've been doing some research. Wouldn't this move preclude me from continuing it?"

"Yes, I suppose it would."

So she didn't want to go, and we didn't go. I involved my wife, my key team member, in the decision, and I'm sure it was the right one. I gave up a bit of career advance for a better marriage and family relationship, and I never regretted it.

In balancing our career and family wants, our family members play a special role in helping us mold and shape our balance, and ultimately help us define what is most important to us.

2. Understand Family Concerns

The familiarity that comes with being a family often allows people to take for granted the formal commitment that is needed to create family balance. Miscommunication leads to faulty assumptions.

Our spouses/partners and children/close relations need to provide their own input as to how the family is functioning from their points of view. How are their needs and perspectives on the family being shaped by our choices?

Our spouses and children might have very different expectations of what *family membership* means to them. If they don't know what we expect of them, they aren't likely to meet our expectations. And if they aren't buying into our expectations of them, they will be violating our expectations regularly.

Or they may have their own ideas about how they can and will contribute to the family. Their creative contributions may take a different form than we anticipated. We may have to shift our view of what constitutes an acceptable and meaningful contribution from them at different times and circumstances in life.

We need to understand what role each family member wants to play in creating balance. Role reversals or adjustments may be needed at times. The provider may become the nurturer for a season. Think of the family as a theater company or cast in live production. Changing conditions may dictate using cast members in novel ways—a lead actor may need to play a supporting role, for example. Or a supporting role player who has matured and gained experience may be ready for a new role.

Sandy is in her late 40s and has been a college professor for the last 20 years. She is enjoying a stable career with relatively predictable hours and is proud of the dialogue she has with her family. Without this dialogue, Sandy feels that she wouldn't have the balance she enjoys at this stage in her life.

SANDY'S STORY

For each of us, balance will have its own nuances, and you must be comfortable with the balance you've found for yourself. You may miss some of your children's significant performances and not be available when they are sick and need to be picked up from school. There may be times when you will be out of town, when some of the most important firsts happen, like a first step or first word—so how can you call this balance?

Is balance simply the ability to get to do what you want with your life and be with your children when it is convenient for you or when you deem it to be the right time? This probably isn't your kids' idea of balance. I'm sure they want Mom or Dad there when they get home from school, or when they want to talk and not to have to call you on the phone. This is all true. They didn't choose this type of balance, although I would definitely say that they have a say in the situation.

I deal with these issues by frequently sitting down as a family and talking about the time we spend together and what each member needs. These conversations sound simple, yet most families do not engage in them. Sometimes all it takes is a few simple questions and answers on a regular basis to understand exactly what our families need and how we might accommodate that.

I have had many surprises during these conversations, learning that my children's and even my husband's time requests are often different than I would have assumed. In fact, they have told me that they don't like it when I come to every one of their games because it makes them nervous, and they don't perform as well. But they love it when I make them breakfast in the mornings.

I recommend talking to your kids to learn what works for them. That's really the only way to know. Schedule meetings with each other regularly to understand what all the different needs are. If you have a weekly meeting with your boss to make sure you're on the same page, why not with your family?

Step 5

Sandy's balancing choices did not reflect what her children defined as balance. She needed to understand how her children viewed things, what was important to them, and how she could meet their needs more effectively. The sessions that Sandy scheduled with her family helped them to understand what she was trying to accomplish. Such sharing is vital to achieve balance. Sandy's story helps us to understand the importance of spending this time with our families as we create our balance.

We encourage you to have regularly scheduled (perhaps weekly) "dialogue sessions" with your family members. Without having some schedule and structure for family dialogue and activity, you may never get around to it.

Also, your understanding of family concerns is greatly facilitated when you are present wherever you are— whether at work or at home. When you are working, work. When you spend time with your family, enjoy it! Kids are very attuned to our presence! Even if we are physically there, they can easily tell if we are not emotionally present.

You can enhance your ability to be emotionally present in the moment by taking time for yourself in order to be fully present with your children. It's a matter of practice, discipline, and meditation.

We must optimize our choices, then have confidence in them. Knowing how much we need of each in order to function best in both is the key to resolving conflicts between our chosen priorities. We need certain time with our families to function well at work. If we have too little time with them, we are thinking of them all the time at work and can't focus. If we have too little time for our careers, things pile up, we fall behind, and our minds may be preoccupied with work while we are with our families.

3. Be Creative in the Way You Spend Time with Your Kids

Family time is a dynamic process. As kids get older, their needs change. The needs of our spouses can also change. How do we keep up?

Just as Sandy explained, meeting regularly with our families enables us to discuss just how these needs are changing. It can also provide a creative forum for generating new ideas of how to engage more effectively with each family member.

By having weekly sessions, we can be more organized in setting our balancing choices, resulting in more genuine, guilt-free time with family. This step can also help keep the activities fun and interesting for each family member.

4. Make Sure that Both Parents are Striving to be Balanced

Each parent needs to have a balance between work and family, individually as well as a couple. Unbalanced parents don't make for a balanced marriage or family.

Don't assume that if each parent is unbalanced in a different way—one for career and the other for family—the family is balanced. The key is for each parent to be balanced, then to work together to be balanced as a team. Because the truth is:

Two unbalanced parents don't make a balanced one. Nor can one balanced parent compensate for the imbalance of a mate.

Some parents feel that because one of them can be at home and have dinner every night with the family while the other is at work full time, they have found the solution. They believe that if one parent sacrifices, balance can be achieved.

If both parents work full schedules at their jobs, it seems impossible for them to catch every basketball game or recital, or to always be there for dinner. But this is where having much of what we really want comes into play. We can't have it all—meaning we can't be at every game, every dinner, and every important work meeting—but we can have much of what we want most.

Both parents have to be balanced to have a balanced family. And this requires making critical choices together, as a family, in order for both parents to get a lot of those things that are most important to them.

Illusion: **I can figure out alone what is best for my family.**

Reality: **No matter how well intentioned we are, we can be mistaken about what is most important to those we love and what they really hope for from us.**

Jimmy is in his early 30s. He got married and started a family during the last few years. He met his wife, Clarissa, at the marketing firm where he worked. He discusses the choices and tradeoffs he has made in choosing to be a stay-at-home father

JIMMY'S STORY

Clarissa and I both started on a management track with the same firm. Then we had our first child, and we realized that we couldn't both devote enough time to climb the promotion ladder successfully.

We discussed the situation, and I agreed to stay home a lot with the kids while she devoted herself to her career because she was already in a higher position within our firm. I took a job that allowed me to work at home, and she spends as much time as is required to get ahead at work.

We made this decision to ensure that our family is balanced—that the children get the support of at least one parent at all times, and that at least one of us is able to pursue a career successfully.

Clarissa excels in her field and sees the children when she has time, which isn't very often. I feel her regret in having already missed so much. Although many working parents envy me for being there for every important event in my children's lives, I also feel disappointed that I can't pursue the career goals that I have set for myself. I feel guilty to even feel this way! I love my kids so much and wouldn't want to be away from them as much as Clarissa is away because I know it's not the same thing as being there when you just get the highlights over the phone.

But working from home and taking care of the kids is challenging. Even though I have help from a babysitter during many of the hours, it is very hard to say no when Ruthie wants me to help her with homework. I usually end up working late into the night, and find I have little time to spend on my own. When Clarissa gets home from work, she's exhausted. And since I have been home all day, she doesn't consider that I might need some downtime, as well. It's tough. Neither of us has balance.

Jimmy paints a difficult picture of two parents with the best of intentions, trying to create that perfect balance between a successful career and a loving family. He expresses that it is their priority to give their children undivided attention by at least one parent while the other puts all the efforts into career advancement.

Divide and Conquer?

The idea of "divide and conquer" can be very seducing—one partner taking the left flank while the other takes the right—but this will only leave the two of you exhausted, having fought challenges in two different realms and making it that much more difficult to understand the other's fatigue.

The more effective way to be a team is to create your balance together—help each other find ways to be better balanced.

Follow the steps in these chapters as a unified team and share in the struggles. This will serve to strengthen your ties, not weaken them.

Although the number of stay-at-home fathers is rising, the trend today is still that an overwhelming majority of women are the ones who choose to stay at home.

Choose to be balanced parents together, thus minimizing the regret and guilt that accumulates from being unbalanced.

Critical Success Factors in Refining Your Balance

- Make your family a part of your balancing choice. This is critical to your successful balance.

- Acquaint yourself with the expectations and priorities of each family member.

- Stay in the moment. To balance those things that are most important to you, be aware of where you are—while at home and while at work.

Having It All...and Making It Work

- Find creative ways of meeting the needs of your children and your spouse—and keep these methods updated!

- Permit both parents to achieve balance. This is the only solution to becoming a balanced leader.

Review Your Balance to Retain or Regain It: *Balance Is a Destination*

You may be down or out of balance, but you can learn to recover nicely, especially when you know what knocks you off balance or causes you to slip slowly out of balance. Assess your situation periodically and strive for flexibility. In doing so, you can actually be in balance most of the time.

Some aspects of our lives are always journeys—building and maintaining relationships, deepening love, building our character, enhancing our careers.

Balance, too, at least for different periods in our lives, is a journey. But to say that it is *always* a journey suggests that we never get there—that we never truly achieve balance. Not true.

This Journey Leads to a Destination

Balance is an achievable destination. We can actually get there and not always just be going in its direction. In fact, we *must* get there, because if we're always just pursuing balance but never achieving it, we haven't solved any of the conflicts between work and family that can lead to painful outcomes.

So balance is not a journey but a destination, a sense of being there and staying there, or getting back there if we get knocked out of it or slip out of it unintentionally.

In this chapter, we suggest how we can stay balanced. These tips are intended to keep us at our destination point so that we don't somehow lose balance and get lost! If we fall out of balance, we can start again by remembering how we achieved balance in the first place. This chapter will help us to find our balance again.

The journey is the process we take to achieve balance. Balance is the end point. But the journey is always starting anew, and the end point is always shifting.

What Knocks Us Off Balance

Two things often knock us out of balance. By understanding these and watching for others, we can recognize when they affect our balance and take precautions.

Step 6

The Knock-You-Down Things

Some things can simply knock you down or out of balance through no fault of your own—at least you like to think you are merely an innocent victim of circumstances beyond your control. In some cases, you may well be an innocent victim. Bad things can and do happen. Still, be careful about what you put in this category, because it implies or presumes your innocence or your inability to recover. Being knocked down is not necessarily the same as being knocked out—you can recover. Some of the knock-you-down things that can happen are:

- You suffer an accident, injury, or illness.

- A family member suffers an accident, injury, illness, or death.

- You lose your job or become plateaued at work.

- Your company merges, downsizes, or goes bankrupt.

- You and your spouse are divided, separated, or divorced.

When such things happen, they can knock you out of balance and into a situation where you have to go through the process of achieving balance again. This may happen dozens of times throughout your life. Do not fear the process; every time you do it, it becomes that much easier. If something knocks you out of balance, you must make the journey again.

The Slippery Things

Some things can slip you out of balance, almost without you realizing it. It's like having a slow leak in a tire. You may find more of your time going one way toward something else and not to the things that are most important to you. For example, here are a few of the "slippery things" you may wrestle with:

- Loss of romance in the marital relationship
- Loss of enthusiasm for your work
- Loss of marketability of your product or service
- Loss of profitability of your company
- Overindulgence of a hobby or habit

Review Your Balance

We suggest making periodical assessments to prevent a loss of balance or to minimize the things that slip you out of balance. Ask yourself, What knock-down things and slippery things are causing me balance problems?

You won't be in a state of balance at every moment. There may be times in your life (perhaps lasting decades, not just days) when work takes up more of your time and times in your life when family or personal issues take up more of your time. So you must periodically assess how you are allocating your time to ensure that you are aligned with your balancing choices.

We suggest that you evaluate your balance twice a year as a family to assess life goals and direction, and monthly as an individual to think about the functional, day-to-day aspects of balance.

Here is a simple assessment form:

Monthly Individual Assessment

- What are my priorities?

- How am I currently spending my time?

- What things are falling short or missing?

- What adjustments do I need to make?

Biannual Family Assessment

- What are our family priorities?

- How are we currently spending our time?

- What things are falling short or missing?

- What adjustments do we need to make?

Again, we emphasize the importance of not doubting your balancing choices until your scheduled evaluation time.

Paul, a real estate broker in his mid-50s, has four children and a wife of 27 years. He discusses the actions he took to involve his family in assessing their balance and making adjustments.

PAUL'S STORY

How I keep everything in balance is by having an appointment with my spouse and children written on my calendar. We call it "Balance Day." Every six months, I sit down and look at my priorities, and make some choices about how to spend my time. Then I share these with the family, and we discuss what works for them. I also review it independently every month to make sure I am still on track. I give my attention to different sections of my priority list at different times during the year. I don't think that everything is perfectly clear all the time.

Frequently, I feel somewhat out of balance. But at the checkpoints, when I stop to look back, if things do not look right, I change them. It takes tremendous discipline, but I can live with the daily imbalance as long as I continuously question and am satisfied with the overall picture. The whole family does this, then we share our goals with each other and try to weave them together as much as possible.

Paul now takes time individually to assess his balance, in addition to holding review sessions with his family. The process to achieving balance is not perfect; it will take patience and fine-tuning. Perhaps it may take many reviews before the multiple aspects of our balance seem just right. By periodically assessing our progress, we avoid the subtle things that slowly slip us out of balance and ensure that we are getting a lot of those things that we want most.

Illusion: **I can find balance in my life and just stay there.**

Reality: **The circumstances of our lives and those of our loved ones are always changing, so we have to adapt our efforts at balance continually.**

Learn to Be Flexible

We can't know how the choices we make at each critical juncture will impact our ability to meet our balancing goals. This means we need to be flexible, adjust, and refine our balance.

Be cautious about planning life too rigidly. Creating balance requires us to adjust our priority list periodically. Both our work and family lives are dynamic, so something that works today might not work next week. We must rework our balance when new and important things come up suddenly and require us to reorder our priorities. This does not mean that what we were doing was wrong; it simply means that there needs to be a degree of flexibility when balancing our family and work.

Flexibility—The Crucial Rule of this Game

If we are like a great oak tree with strong roots and a thick trunk, we may be too inflexible to bend when the wind blows at gale force. We need to be like the sapling that bends when the wind blows; after all, we can control only so many things—and the wind of change isn't one of them.

So how can we be pliant with priorities? Again, we need to assess priorities periodically against the winds of current events and conditions.

Don't Miss Your Opportunity

We can't afford to wait to be balanced. To procrastinate is to prolong our imbalance and invite disaster.

Peter is an executive in his mid-50s who graduated from one of top business schools and led Fortune 500 companies for most of his career. He has three children and has been married to his wife for 32 years. He came to speak to Harvard Business School students to warn them about how easy it is to ignore our need for balance, resulting in tough choices that may have otherwise been avoidable. His is a story about how a person was able to reevaluate his own life after many years, to realize that he had lost balance between his career and his family so that he wasn't fulfilling his key priorities, then was able to change his life to gain real balance for the first time.

PETER'S STORY

Ever since I was in college, I wanted to be CEO of a large public company, and I went after it hard. I got married about seven years after graduating from college. I decided to start my family at that point, even though I was still very committed to my career. I had met and married the perfect woman for me, and we both wanted to have children right away. I figured that sooner or later I'd get around to having more time for my children.

I didn't let anything divert me from my course—not my marriage, not my children when they came along, not my religion—nothing. My plan was to make it to the top, then take a break and devote some time to my family. I put in six, often seven days a week at the office, and I was out of town more than half the nights of the year.

My focus worked quite well for me. I reached the very top of my company and led it to many successes. Plus, I was the provider for my family, because my wife didn't work. I wanted to provide them with as many resources as I could, so that's what I did.

For the beginning of my children's lives, I was completely absorbed in my work, and before I knew it, my oldest was a teenager. When I finally took a pause to look around, my wife was threatening to divorce me. I realized that I was still going full force in my career, but I was losing my family in the process.

The time frames in my strategy weren't working as I'd planned. Life, for some reason, decided not to abide by my plan. Something had to give, or I was going to lose my family altogether.

It was a frightening moment for me when, at a school conference, my daughter's teacher slipped a piece of paper to me. She had a very serious look on her face. Written on the paper was a poem entitled "Why Is Daddy Never There?" and it was about me—how I wasn't there to kiss her knee when she scraped it or give her advice when she was having trouble with friends or homework.

She couldn't figure out why I wasn't there. Reading this poem was one of the saddest moments of my life. Suddenly, I couldn't figure out why I hadn't been there. It was certainly a wakeup call. When I read my daughter's poem, I was in line to be the next CEO at a company that had just purchased my previous company. In fact, it was a tremendous effort for me to even get to that teacher's conference. I had wanted to be CEO of a big company all my life, and now I was about to get it. There was another candidate, but I was sure I would win the job—I'm still sure. But there I was with this poem and with my wife telling me that I wouldn't have a family if I took the job. She asked me how many nights a year I'd be away. I was sure I would be gone over half the year, but I couldn't tell her.

I realized that if I got the job, it might mean losing my family. I had already made good money; I didn't need to work. I felt like I was being forced to choose between my career and my family. I agonized over the matter for weeks; I talked with my wife about it frequently. I had to make up my mind, and I had to be comfortable with what I decided.

Finally I made a decision. I decided to remove my name from consideration for the CEO job. Conflicting emotions coursed through me. I knew that if I did that, it would end my career. And it did. Once I was out of the line for succession, people stopped coming to me.

Soon a reorganization occurred, and the other candidate for CEO was promoted to a position over me. Suddenly I was reporting to him, and he and I didn't see eye to eye. I didn't like the direction he was taking the company, I wasn't comfortable with his leadership style, and I disagreed with his ethics.

Six months later, I resigned. Suddenly I was in unfamiliar territory. For years I'd been devoted to my career first. The company was really my life. Now it was gone, or rather I was gone from it. I was afraid I'd lost myself.

But I quickly discovered many other things life has to offer. I realized that I could still live a complete life without being CEO, and I still had a few years left to get to know my children before they left for college. I had been successful in my career, and it was time to reach out to my family. I joined a small investment company where I have lots of time for my family.

I've watched many of my peers who have pursued their careers to the end, getting the CEO position, and also usually a divorce. They're often full of regret. When we were young, we didn't think at all of these things. We just started our careers and pushed as hard as we could to climb the career ladder. We got married on the way, but we didn't ever spend enough time with our spouses or our children. Then we each woke up one day to find ourselves successful in business but missing much of life.

It's a sad thing to be fifty years old and full of regret for what can't be regained or made right.

Peter's story is dramatic and unusual, in that he reached almost the top of his profession, then turned away. Most people don't rise so high, nor at the last moment change their minds about what is most important to them. But his story is not unusual in his expression of regret for how his life worked out. Peter's struggle to balance his family and career ambitions is all too real—and it highlights our own vulnerability. Although later in his life, Peter could see that he was on the wrong track and could then make better choices to balance his family and career, many people never reach this realization until it's too late.

Having It All...and Making It Work

It's not that Peter was on the wrong career track but that he was not exercising balance along the way.

When asked about his experience, Peter is thoughtful and certain. "A person can't have both the goal to be a CEO and be fair to his or her family. There isn't enough time in the day; there isn't enough focus in a person's heart."

When we are young, we think we can have a completely successful career and a wonderful family. We think that we see examples of older people around us who are successful at both. We set out to achieve both. We generally don't run into people like Peter, who tell us that there's a major tradeoff—that total success in a career is often gained at the cost of one's family life, and vice versa.

When we asked Peter why some business people in certain careers contend that they do, in fact, have it all, he told us that it's similar to how adults deceive children about Santa Claus—successful business people insist they have it all, even when they don't.

Why do they do that? Perhaps because they don't want to admit to the sacrifices they've made, fearing that other people will think less of them. But the sacrifices are no less real for not being acknowledged—at least, that's Peter's message to us. So most people face a similar dilemma: to be committed to a career, sacrificing personal relationships; or to be committed to personal relationships, sacrificing a career.

Step 6

Balance gives you the chance to have both—so don't waste the opportunity. Having it all doesn't mean getting everything that anyone can imagine—it means having a lot of the things that are really important to us and knowing what is most important and how to get lots of those things.

We are each pressured to embody society's vision of success—of what it means to have it all. The greatest service we can do is to be authentically true to ourselves by accepting that we can't have or be it all. Don't try to be Julia Child in the kitchen, Martha Stewart in the living room, George Soros on the trading floor, Don Juan in the bedroom, and Michael Johnson on the running track. Leaders often struggle in all aspects of their lives to embody the very best.

We can't possibly be superstars in everything. We are who we are. And we need to be satisfied with that. We must choose to balance those aspects that define who we are—to find and balance the unique combination of wants and needs that is authentically ourselves. And of course, in all of this, we must accept that what we want may not be the same as anyone else, and that is absolutely fine.

Achieving balance is not easy to do, but when you're achieving a new and better quality of life, your life is so much better. Sure, making these changes might be awkward at first, but in the end it's worth it. The balanced approach brings us peace of mind.

The evidence is the lives of people all about us. People get involved in infidelity, addictions, obsessions, compulsions, poor lifestyles or physical habits, poor communication and relationship skills, marital problems, money mismanagement, and fraud. Many people say that these things are causing imbalance in their lives. They aren't. Many of the dysfunctional elements of people's lives are the symptoms of a lack of balance, not its cause. But like so many symptoms, once they get started, they can be as bad as the cause.

So the way to deal with disrupters is at the outset. Don't let your life get out of balance. Follow the steps in this book to keep in balance, and these awful symptoms that ruin so many other people's lives and make ever getting back to balance so difficult are very unlikely to happen to you.

Through balance, being a successful professional makes you a better parent, and being a better parent makes you a more effective professional. Work and family reinforce one another. When there's no friction between the two, there's no tension, guilt, or regret. We're better at our jobs, and we're better with our family. And we're at peace with ourselves as effective, happy, balanced leaders.

Step 6

Your Back-to-Balance Plan

Balance is a destination that you can get to, usually within six months, if you follow the process. If you are all career and no family, you may need more time. If you are all family and no career, you may also need more time to get there.

Why not take a moment now to draft your own six-month *back-to-balance plan*? In your plan, apply the six steps we recommend They are summarized at the end of this book.

If you are trying to have a family and a career with a good start in each—and struggling with the tension between the two—you now have a process for achieving balance in a relatively short time if you really go after it.

By following the tips in this chapter, you can become balanced: You can refine it, improve it, remain in balance for longer periods, and regain your balance faster when you do get knocked down.

We are destined to be balanced people, and many of us will learn to be balanced leaders.

Critical Success Factors to the Destination of Balance

■   Remember that this journey leads to a destination.

■   Beware of the knock-you-out things.

■ Flexibility is crucial.

■ Review your balance periodically and have a back-to-balance plan to regain it when it is lost.

Six Steps to Career/ Family Balance

Step 1. Commit to Wanting Both a Career and Family: *Rethinking Your Priorities*

■ You can have career and family in the same time frame. Don't postpone one past its rightful time for the other.

■ The leadership challenge requires us to define our balance.

Illusion: **We can fulfill our career goals and our family goals at separate times during our lives.**

Reality: **Career and family should be done simultaneously. If we sacrifice our career goals to satisfy our family goals, we are not balanced. If we focus on our career at the expense of our families, we are not balanced.**

Critical Success Factors

■ Think hard about what you really value and what you really want.

■ Take responsibility for being proactive about attaining and maintaining balance.

■ Make a list of priorities that clarify what is most important in work and home life, and be sure there's time for them.

Step 2. Pursue a Process that Creates Balance: *Balancing What Is Most Important to You*

■ Establish boundaries early on.

■ Know your priorities.

■ Be satisfied with your choices.

■ Define success on your own terms.

Illusion: **Balance will create itself.**

Reality: **Take responsibility to pursue your own balance proactively. Don't wait for someone else, such as your boss or your spouse, to provide balance for you.**

Critical Success Factors

■ Create balance: It will not emerge without effort and it cannot simply be stumbled upon.

■ Stick by the decisions you make. Once you make your choices, be satisfied with them.

- Reduce guilt and anxiety that results from second-guessing yourself.

- Benchmarking your success externally results in a never-ending cycle in which the more you see, the more you want.

- Balance frees you to be happy with what you have.

Step 3. Make Choices and Accept the Consequences: *Giving Up What You Don't Want Badly Enough*

- Clear the decks to minimize the tradeoffs.

- Learn to say no without feeling guilty.

- Make critical choices that permit attaining balance and accept the consequences of those choices.

Illusion: We can make up later in life for what we've put aside earlier.

Reality: We can't make up later in life for what we've put aside earlier. If we focus on our careers at the expense of our families, missing our children growing up, we'll never get that back. Conversely, if we drop off the career track to raise families, it's almost impossible to get back on; thus, we'll miss the opportunity to achieve our career goals.

Critical Success Factors

■ Balance is about getting as much of our families and careers as we can. This means we must minimize the tradeoffs between them.

■ Tradeoffs are always a win-lose situation because you're choosing between your first priorities.

■ When we are choosing between the things we want most and things that aren't as important, we aren't making tradeoffs. When you give up something of secondary importance to get something of major importance, you dispense with second-tier priorities—that's a win, not a tradeoff.

■ Clear the decks of second-tier items to make room for those things that you want most.

- Letting go of the things you don't want badly enough shouldn't result in any guilt when you say no.

- If you don't clearly know what is most important to you, you may make the wrong choices.

Step 4. Choose a Career that Supports Balance: *Making Your Balance Real*

- Choose your career path wisely.
- Make balancing decisions about your career.
- Use key career levers.

Illusion: **I can choose whatever job or career I like best without regard to my family, and I can somehow find time for my family, too.**

Reality: **We have to choose our jobs and careers carefully to be sure they permit us to have enough time for our families.**

Critical Success Factors

■ Not all careers provide the possibility for balance: We must choose careers in which balancing actions are possible.

■ If we don't have balance in our current work situation, we can try to change the corporate culture of our current job, move laterally within the organization, or if all else fails, leave.

■ Lateral job movement can be a good tool in achieving balance in our current working environment.

■ Try to manage the culture of our workplace by proactively taking action that involves our bosses and colleagues.

■ Don't be afraid to leave current employment if we aren't given the space to create balance; otherwise, we risk ending up with regret for all the things we've missed.

■ When making a new career decision, take into account the major aspects that influence our ability to balance; then choose wisely with balance in mind.

Step 5. Involve Your Loved Ones in Creating Balance: *Refining Your Balance*

- It's important to involve all team members.

- Understanding family paradigms.

- Be present where you are—whether at work or at home.

- Be creative in the way you spend time with your kids.

- Make sure both parents strive to be balanced.

Illusion: **I can figure out alone what is best for my family.**

Reality: **No matter how well intentioned we are, we can be mistaken about what is most important to those we love and what they really hope for from us.**

Critical Success Factors

- Make your family a part of your balancing choices. It's too easy to rationalize your choices, and your families will help keep you from making serious mistakes.

■ Get acquainted with the expectations and priorities of each family member.

■ Stay in the moment. To balance a lot of the things that are most important to you, be aware of where you are—when at home, focus on family; when at work, focus on work.

■ Find creative ways of meeting the needs of your children and your spouse—and keep these methods updated!

■ Expect yourself and your partner to achieve balance. This is the only solution to finding balance for yourself. You can't balance your relationships by unbalancing your loved ones.

Step 6. Review Your Balance to Retain or Regain It: *Balance Is a Destination*

■ Balance is an achievable destination.

■ Review periodically because you can get knocked off balance.

■ Flexibility is crucial.

■ Have a back-to-balance plan.

Illusion: I can find balance in my life and just stay there.

Reality: The circumstances of our lives and those of our loved ones are always changing, so we have to adapt our efforts at balance continually.

Critical Success Factors

- Remember that this journey leads to a destination.
- Beware of the knock-you-out things.
- Flexibility is crucial to good balance.
- Review your balance periodically and have a back-to-balance plan to regain it when it is lost.

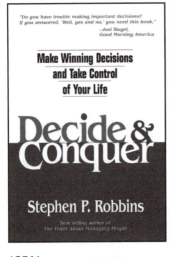